# Understanding
# CATHOLICISM

EXPLANATIONS OF THE CATHOLIC CHURCH
FOR NON-CATHOLIC CHRISTIANS
AND FALLEN AWAY CATHOLICS

# HUGH MURRAY

ISBN-13: 978-1983383557

Cover design by Ellen Meyer and Vicki Lesage

*To my loving and supportive wife, Mary Ellen Grohar-Murray, and to my uncle, Dr. Joseph B. Grindon, who encouraged (i.e., prodded) me to attend Catholic discussion meetings in the late 1960's. These meetings were well planned by Jesuits and attended by highly informed Catholic men, and they stimulated a lifelong interest in learning more about all things Catholic.*

# TABLE OF CONTENTS

# INTRODUCTION

This book provides a brief explanation of key Catholic facts and concepts designed for readers who already have a belief in Jesus Christ. For purposes of this book, belief in Jesus Christ requires belief in a person:

a) who lived in Judea some 2,000 years ago
b) who is one person possessed of two natures, human and divine
c) who is the second person of a Triune God
d) who is the person who suffered and died so that mankind might be saved from the consequence of their sins
e) who rose from the dead to fulfill the Old Testament prophecies and dispel doubt about His role as Saviour and Messiah.

This book is not intended to be argumentative or designed to win converts to the Catholic faith. There will, of course, be statements herein that might conflict with one or more belief statements of one or more other Christian Churches. Again these statements are not being made to be argumentative but simply to illuminate the Catholic view of matters.

This book is simply intended to convey information and understanding to those who already possess a love of Jesus Christ, their God and Saviour, and who are simply interested in learning something about how another large Christian denomination, the Catholic Church, celebrates Christ's redeeming, saving acts through its liturgy and practices.

Because of its limited scope, this book will not attempt to bring the reader to a belief in the existence of God, nor to a belief in Christ as man's Saviour.

# PART I – CATHOLIC BELIEFS AND TRADITIONS

# A Catholic View of God, Man, and Man's Relationship with God

Catholics view God as the only independent entity in existence; everything else and every other person is dependent for their or its existence on God. Without God's active will holding these things and persons in existence these would cease to exist. God is infinitely possessed of all qualities (e.g., knowledge, good, truth, love, power, etc.). God even uses his infinite power to hold in existence that which is opposed to Him such as fallen angels (e.g., devils) and men possessed of deeply wicked intentions (e.g., Hitler, Stalin, Mao, etc.). God exists outside of any restraint including time. For God all of history is immediately present to him.

There are three persons in the Godhead, and they all possess the same perfect, unified nature. This assures that the three persons, Father, Son and Holy Spirit, always act in perfect harmony. Some details about the Trinity have been revealed, but most details of the Trinity's operation are a mystery.

Catholics believe God has let man know about his existence by setting before man a creation which attests to

God's existence and by sending the Son, Jesus Christ, to fulfil the prophesy recorded in the Old Testament and to redeem all people giving them a way to deal with their sins.

Man is the only creature created by God who has been given a conscience (i.e., an innate sense of good and evil), a free will (i.e., the ability to choose the good or the evil), an ability to know about birth and death, and the ability to learn acquiring knowledge to increase understanding, etc.

Man's possession of free will combined with his ability to grow in knowledge puts man in a position of knowing about God and choosing to love God. Of course, man by himself is incapable of steadfastness in his love of God or his rejection of sin. God realizing man's fallen position following the sin of Adam and Eve sent his Son, Jesus Christ, to become a man and to die in reparation for each man's sins and to set forth a way for God's grace to flow to man so man would have the strength to rise above his propensity to sin.

Accordingly, Catholics believe, Christ created a Church, the Catholic Church, which was to provide a way for God's grace to flow to people via the seven Sacraments, created by Christ, which the Catholic Church administers through its ordained clergy. (See the section on "the Sacraments" below.) In addition to this Sacramental Grace, Catholics believe that baptized persons, who are free of serious sin, can also receive Actual Grace for their prayers and good works.

Additionally, Catholics believe man is "made in the image and likeness of God." This belief stems from the fact that man possesses, in an imperfect, partial way, many qualities which God possesses in a perfect, infinite way. For instance, man has the ability to love, albeit imperfectly, while God's love for man and all creation is a perfect love.

# History – The First Thousand Years

Catholics believe that Christ ordained the existence of a Church when he said to Peter, "Upon this rock I will build my church." This fact lies behind the 2,000-year history of the Catholic Church headed by a string of successors to Peter, called Popes.

The Church, in the decades following Christ's Ascension, had to deal with heresy and questions of morally correct behavior. During the first 400 years there was no New Testament or Bible. There were various writings circulating about Jesus and his apostles. However, these various Gospels and other documents did not provide detailed guidance on many things. So during this period the church decided on a system to implement Jesus' plan called the Councilor system, where church leaders (e.g., the Pope and bishops) would meet and decide what the Church's position would be on questions of faith (beliefs) and morals (acceptable behavior). For instance, the apostles had to deal with the question of whether gentiles could become Christians without first becoming Jews. This had to be decided so the Apostles had a meeting to decide the issue under the guidance of Peter. (Acts 15)

During this 400-year period, Christianity grew from a few hundred believers in Asia Minor, to a large, though persecuted, religious sect found in many cities of the Empire, to finally a fully tolerated religion accepted across the Roman Empire. The most significant event in this process occurred in 312 just a few days before the Battle of Milivian Bridge just north of Rome. The attacking force was led by Constantine (b.272 - d.337) who had a dream in which Christ appeared with a cross and said to Constantine, "With this sign, you will conquer." Constantine had his forces place images of the cross on their shields and helmets. At the battle, they defeated a much larger force led by Maxentius. Constantine went on to become the sole emperor of the entire Roman Empire. In 313 he raised Christianity from the status of a persecuted sect to a fully tolerated religion.

At this time, the majority of Christians were located in the Eastern Roman Empire. As Christians emerged into full recognition, it became apparent that there were doctrinal and liturgical differences in various Christian groups. This led leaders, under the urging of Constantine, to seek standardization.

There were large numbers of Arian heretics who were confusing true Christians about the nature of Christ. They felt Christ was little more than a good man. Clarity was needed.

A council was called at Nicea in 325 to set forth a belief statement or creed for Christians. There was another council held in Constantinople in 381 which refined the Nicene Creed. Basil of Caesarea, Gregory of Nazianzen, and Athanasius of Egypt were particularly active in guiding these Councils. The final result, called the Nicene Creed, has come down to us today as Christianity's basic statement of belief.

Regarding the liturgy, Basil and John Chrysostom were particularly active in creating a standardized liturgy for all

Christians to use. The actual liturgies designed by Basil (two hours in length) and John (a one-hour liturgy), are still celebrated today. Although most liturgies used today are adaptations, they all retain the essential elements set down by Basil and John. (For more on this, see the elements of Mass below.)

As the Western Roman Empire began to unravel in the 5th century, a Christian named Benedict of Nursia decided to organize a group of men at a fixed location who loved Jesus Christ and wished to serve God through a life of "work and prayer." These men also wanted stability in the midst of a newly unstable world. More and more of these groups of men living at fixed locations began to appear. These places were called Benedictine Abbeys and the men living there were called Benedictine monks. These places were stable and became the repositories of not only Christian knowledge, but also of Roman, Greek, and other knowledge. Accordingly, schools sprang up in these locations. So monks not only grew crops and performed the necessary crafts for daily living, but they also become educators of future generations.

This councilor system was augmented by the official certification of a standardized New Testament with 27 books in 393 AD. This was done in steps. First the documents were selected by the Synod of Hippo and then the Council of Rome. These documents were to be attached to the Jewish scriptures, which Christians call the Old Testament, to create the first Bible. Second, the Pope engaged a great linguist and Latin stylist named Jerome (b.~340-d.420) to compile the books of the entire Bible into well-written standard Latin. Where acceptable Latin versions were not available, Jerome had to do a Latin translation from scratch. Jerome's finished product was called the Vulgate. For the next 1,000 years monks carefully hand copied the Vulgate again and again working to provide every church in Western Europe with a copy.

Beyond Jerome, three others deserve particular mention for their contribution in this era. Ambrose, bishop of Milan, (b.340-d.397) was a student of scriptures. He gave scholarly expositions on the scriptures and people came great distances to hear him preach and have conversations with him. One person who came was Augustine of Hippo (b.354-d.430), an unhappy member of the Manichean heresy, who was seeking knowledge of Christianity.

Augustine was highly educated and was a great speaker and debater; he was impressed with Ambrose and after his questions were answered by Ambrose he became a Christian and returned home. In Hippo, North Africa, he was not allowed to be a retiring Christian content to pray, study and write. The people understanding his wisdom and speaking ability insisted he become their bishop. In that capacity he gave long, enlightening, and entertaining sermons and wrote several letters, books, etc.

About a century later, a high-born Benedictine monk was elevated to Pope. This man became known as Gregory the Great (b.540-d.604). He did many important things:

a)  He made it clear that the Pope was the leader of the bishops and not simply one among equals.

b)  He established Benedict's guiding rules, governing the lives of monks, as the standard rule for all monasteries.

c)  He asked monasteries to encourage some of their healthy monks to leave their monasteries and travel into pagan areas, converting the tribes that had conquered the Roman world.

d)  He standardized the Chants used in Benedictine Abbeys.

e)  He arranged for the wide distribution of Jerome's Vulgate and the ideas in Augustine's work *The City of God.*

These four—Jerome, Ambrose, Augustine, and Gregory—are considered by Catholics to be the four early

Christians who most shaped the development of western Christianity as it entered the Middle Ages.

Even after the Bible was created, the Councilor system continued to provide a means to apply Christ's teachings with appropriate precision to questions of faith and morals. These Councilor statements were binding on Catholics. Additionally there were other statements by the Popes, individual bishops, and scholars which, while important, were not binding on Catholics. Some of these non-binding statements became very important guides for future Church thinking. All these documents, particularly those authored by Popes, comprise the Magisterium, or tradition, of the Catholic Church and provide guidance for all people on hundreds of issues involving faith and morals.

## The First Big Historic Split

In the 700-1000 AD period differences developed between Rome and Constantinople. There was contention over which side of the Church—eastern or western—would send missionaries to convert the Slavic peoples located south of the Baltic Sea and north of the Black Sea and Danube River, and over the hubris of the western church which had arbitrarily changed the Nicene formulation regarding the Holy Spirit.

The original formulation had "the Holy Spirit proceeding from the Father," while the revised formulation had the Holy Spirit proceeding "from the Father and the Son." Constantinople was the home of the most important bishop in the Eastern Church, and Rome was the home of the successor of Peter. However, the Roman emperors had moved the capital of the empire to Constantinople; while Rome, and the western empire, had fallen on hard times due to repeated invasions by pagan tribes. There developed a basic disagreement over what special prerogatives the successors of Peter, the Pope in Rome, would have over all parts of the Church. This came to a head in 1054 when there were reciprocal excommunications of leaders on both sides that split the Church. This split remains in place to this day.

Following this split, the western Church under the successors of Peter went into a period of moral decline. Several Popes were elected who were corrupt, and bishops used their power to feather the nests of their illegitimate children. The Papacy was moved for several decades to Avignon (1309-1377) where it fell under French domination. Additionally, during this period the population suffered through the Black Death and the One Hundred Years War between England and France.

There were trends which countered all this disruption and corruption. One was the Crusades which, though it caused much death and dislocation in the Holy Land, bolstered Western Europe's enthusiasm for the faith from the 11th century to the 14th century. The second was the appearance of the two great mendicant orders, the Franciscans, founded by Francis of Assisi (b.1181-b.1226), and Dominicans, founded by Dominic Guzman (b.1179-b.1221). The men of these orders moved around living lives of self-denial and dedication to the faith. The Dominicans, also called the Order of Preachers, travelled about instructing the faithful, teaching in schools, and debating heretics. Franciscans lived lives of extreme self-denial begging for food and clothing from the rich in the morning and distributing these items in poor neighborhoods in the afternoon. The third was the explosion of beautiful art and architecture (e.g., gothic cathedrals) which helped people raise their minds and hearts to their heavenly Father.

In the middle of the 13th century a heresy, the Albigensian Heresy (or Catharism), emerged in southern

France and northern Italy which held that all things of this world were bad and all good was located only in heaven. To combat this heresy the Catholic Church first used military campaigns but later Church leaders created a process called the Inquisition. Under this process heretics were called in and subjected to interrogation and—if needed—torture to get them to forswear their error. If the heretic persisted in heresy, they could be put to death. This Inquisition process was even more widely used as Christians completed the re-conquest of the Iberian peninsula (1492) from the Muslims. Once Christians regained control, both Muslims and Jews were subjected to the Inquisition and were given the option to emigrate to Morocco, become Christian, or die. Many Muslims and Jews wanting to keep their homes forswore their former beliefs in public but continued to practice their faiths in private. This left the Inquisition with a multi-century task of attempting to identify and deal with these private heretics. The last execution by the Inquisition occurred in the first quarter of the 19th century. It is estimated that about 5,000 people were executed by the Inquisition in the period 1525 to 1825 in the Iberian peninsula.

## The Second Big Historic Split

However, many bishops and some of the Popes continued their corruption, devising schemes to strip money out of the faithful by such things as selling indulgences. These excesses triggered response from such men as Martin Luther (b.1483-d.1546), a priest in Germany, who objected to the corruption. Luther posted his objections on the door of a church in Wittenberg, Germany.

The Catholic hierarchy attempted to capture and punish

Luther, but he was protected by the local royalty. He lived in their various castles and during this time he translated the Bible into German and arranged to get his work printed using the new printing press invented by Gutenberg. This allowed Bibles to be in every home rather than every Church as had formerly been the case.

Luther initially thought the Catholic Church would accept his suggested reforms and that he would end his career as a priest restored to full union with Rome. It was not to be, and Lutheranism grew out of this split.

Following Luther were John Calvin (b.1509-d.1564) of Switzerland and then King Henry VIII of England (b.1491-d.1547). These splits continued and continued until the world had hundreds—indeed thousands—of stand-alone denominations and even unaffiliated "single church" communities.

As these splits began to spread there was conflict between Catholics and Protestants. This led to a devastating war that went on for about thirty years until the Treaty of Westphalia in 1648. (To comprehend the intensity of this war, consider that it is estimated that one third of Germany's population was lost.) This treaty and other later agreements basically allowed people to believe and practice as they wished, but the religion of the monarch would be the official religion of the domain. This led to Lutheranism in northern Germany and Scandinavia, Anglicanism in England, Calvinism or Presbyterianism in Switzerland, Scotland, and Northern Ireland, and so forth.

## The Catholic Church Begins to Reform

Following the successful establishment of Protestantism in large areas of Europe, the Catholics got more serious about reform. A new religious order of highly educated Catholic priests was organized in the 1540's by Ignatius Loyola (b.1491-d.1556) to counter the spread of Protestantism. This order, called the Jesuits, established colleges across Europe where young Catholic men could be properly educated in the Faith. Additionally, the Jesuits sent missionaries to remote areas where Christianity was unknown and great preachers into Protestant areas in Europe to bring people back to the Catholic faith.

Jesuits lacked respect for some local clergy who were poorly educated or used their positions to extract money and favors from the faithful. The presence of Jesuits brought a movement toward greater Catholic reform across Europe.

The final step in this reform process was brought about by the democratizing tendency in various countries. The Church was persecuted and, after some push back, it had to accommodate itself to these new governments. The Church lost its temporal, political control of central Italy and eventually was forced into a small area of a few hundred acres where the Vatican is located today.

The Councilor System of Church governance fell into disuse from 1580 until 1870. During this time the Pope was accommodating to outside events and major political change. However, in 1870 the Pope decided to ask the bishops assembled in a council, called Vatican I, to formally give all Popes the power to declare certain beliefs regarding faith and morals as binding on Catholics. The bishops at Vatican I voted to formally give the Pope this right, even though most Catholics had attributed this power to the Popes for many centuries.

The next council, called Vatican II, was a pastoral council designed to renew the Church. This council was not called to adjust beliefs in faith and morals, rather it was designed to engage the faithful in the Church. The only change to faith and morals was a less stringent standard for being saved. Prior to Vatican II, Catholics held that for those who knew about the Catholic Church salvation was only available by joining the Catholic Church. After Vatican II, Catholics believed salvation was available to non-Catholics through their own religious traditions or communities.

# Mass and Other Sacraments

The Catholic Church teaches that there are seven Sacraments instituted by Christ. Each is signified by an outward sign which conveys inwardly sacramental grace to the recipient, said grace having been earned for mankind by Christ on the cross.

The Mass, otherwise known as the Holy Eucharist, is the most frequently received sacrament. This sacrament was instituted by Christ at the Last Supper when he required the apostles to "do this in remembrance of me." The Mass, as it has evolved, is a re-enactment of the Last Supper, a sacrificial offering to God the Father, and a bloodless re-enactment of Christ's sacrifice on the Cross.

In the ancient world, people regularly offered sacrifices. The concept of sacrifice to their god(s) was a major part of their lives and thinking. For moderns it is useful to think about the idea of offering the "best we have" to God to show our love for and allegiance to Him.

The Sacrifice of the Mass is divided into two major parts:

a) The Liturgy of the Word begins with everyone acknowledging orally that they are sinners; then scripture selections from the Old Testament, the New Testament, and always the Gospels are read and commented on by the priest/celebrant or a deacon. This part of Mass ends with the recitation of the Nicene Creed which is the statement of belief adopted at the Council of Nicaea in 325 AD.

b)  The Liturgy of the Eucharist follows. In this part of the Mass several things occur. First the priest prepares bread and wine for the coming consecration, and he engages in an outward cleansing of hands as he asks God to make him worthy to say this Mass. Then the congregation asks God to sanctify the coming proceedings. Next the priest consecrates the bread and wine, changing them, through the process of transubstantiation, into the Body and Blood of Jesus Christ. At this point, the congregation has the most important thing in its midst that they could possibly possess, namely the Body and Blood of Christ. Then the priest makes a non-bloody offering of Christ's Body and Blood to God the Father asking Him to recall Christ's bloody sacrifice on the cross for our sins. The priest then asks God the Father to look not upon the sins of those gathered but rather on the perfection of Christ which is being offered to Him at this time. The next part of the Mass is the recitation of the Lord's Prayer, and a mutual greeting of people adjunct to each other in the congregation with the term "peace be with you." Finally the congregation, after professing again their sinfulness and unworthiness to receive, goes to Communion. Some receive only the host, others receive under both species. Catholics believe that Christ is fully present in each species.

The Mass ends with the priest's blessing and his command sending the faithful forth "to love and serve" God and your neighbor. For centuries all Masses were said in Latin. In Latin, the verb "to send" is "missa"; this is the source of the English word Mass.

The other sacraments are Reconciliation (Penance), Baptism, Matrimony, the Anointing of the Sick, Holy Orders, and Confirmation.

The most important of all seven Sacraments is Baptism, which initiates a person into the Christian life. It is the sacrament that is most widely shared among all Christian Churches. Catholics believe Baptism can be performed on infants or adults by pouring water on the forehead by a baptized person, not necessarily a priest or deacon, saying "I baptize thee in the name of the Father, the Son, and the Holy Spirit." It should be noted that in non-emergency situations this Sacrament is administered by a priest or deacon at the family's parish church.

Catholics believe that those who die for the Faith, before they are Baptized with water, receive Baptism by blood. In similar fashion, an isolated person who recognizes the work of a "master mind" in the functioning of the world and sincerely desires to align himself with that "master mind" receives the Baptism by desire.

The sacrament received most frequently by Catholics following Communion at Mass is Reconciliation which grows out of Christ's instruction to his apostles "whose sin you shall forgive they are forgiven, whose sin you shall retain they are retained." This instruction requires that the priest know what sins are being confessed. Thus the need for privacy as the penitent discloses his sins. The priest then reviews the sins asking for appropriate clarifications and making suggestions on how sins, particularly repetitive sins, might be avoided. The priest might also point out that a sin can't be forgiven until some act of restitution is performed. If all the sins are ready for forgiveness the priest will ask for an oral statement of contrition that must include sorrow for offending God and the statement that the penitent intends to reform their life, avoiding these sins in the future.

Following that the priest, acting under Christ's injunction, forgives the penitent's sin(s) and assigns a penance (usually the saying of certain prayers for a number of days or performing some charitable act.) A practicing Catholic usually receives this sacrament three or four times per year. The Church teaches there are mortal and venial sins and that Communion may be received worthily if the communicant has only unconfessed venial sins, but that Reconciliation is required before receiving communion if the communicant has an unconfessed mortal sin. A mortal sin involves:

a)   the full engagement of the will
b)   a serious matter
c)   a willful disregard of the offence given to God by the sinful act.

Mortal sins are not easy to commit.

The Sacrament of Matrimony is administered by the couple to each other with this process generally following a proscribed format, in an approved place, before witnesses including a priest or deacon.

The sacrament of the Anointing of the Sick is conducted for individuals facing a serious medical procedure or about to die or even those who have died within an hour or two. The sacrament is also given in group settings where several people are gathered that have serious chronic conditions that might cause sudden death or where people are already diagnosed as being beyond medical help (e.g., in a hospice.)

The sacrament of Confirmation is administered by a bishop (or his priest designee.) The reception of this sacrament requires that the person possess considerable knowledge of the Catholic Church, its history, and its doctrines. The baptized person who receives Confirmation becomes a soldier for Christ, that is someone who is prepared to defend the Catholic faith.

The sacrament of Holy Orders is administered by a bishop and it empowers the selected person, always a man, to perform the Sacraments, particularly to say the Mass and hear confessions. The sacrament of Holy Orders is dispensed in two steps: first the candidate receives the right to perform only five sacraments, leaving out Holy Orders and Confirmation. Later if a priest is selected to become a bishop he receives, through his second ordination, the right to perform the other two sacraments.

# Apostolic Succession

Catholics believe that Christ selected from his many followers 12 apostles who became the first bishops, and that he identified one of the 12, Peter, to be the first Pope. The process of picking additional bishops began, after Judas disqualified himself, when Matthias was selected by the remaining 11 to be the 13th apostle.

This process of picking successors has continued over the years until today there are several thousand bishops serving in nearly every corner of the globe. Every priest and bishop can trace his ordination back through the centuries to one of the 12 apostles and thus to Christ. (This statement is also true for every Orthodox priest. This is why a Catholic in an emergency can go to confession to an Orthodox priest and vice versa.)

# The Special Role of Mary

Catholics assign to Mary a special place of honor. Catholics believe that Mary herself was conceived without the taint of original sin so that her womb would be a fit home for Jesus before his birth. Later Mary, after a long earthly life, was assumed into heaven so she might be with her Son and take up her duties as Queen of Heaven. Since Christ possessed two natures, human and divine, in one person, and since Mary was the mother of the one person, Jesus Christ, she has to be considered the Mother of God. Finally, because Jesus said to John shortly before his death to consider Mary his mother, by extension Catholics feel Mary should be considered everyone's mother as well.

The Rosary has been a very popular devotion for Catholics for the last thousand years. This devotion involves the saying of five decades. Each decade includes one "Our Father" followed by ten "Hail Marys." Each of the five decades said are dedicated to a different but related set of events. For instance, the Five Sorrowful Mysteries are in order: the Agony in the Garden, the Scourging at the Pillar, the Crowning with Thorns, Christ Carrying the Cross, and the Crucifixion. The idea is to say the mystery first visualizing the scene, then saying one "Our Father" followed by the ten "Hail Marys."

The Rosary is generally said by the person holding a set of Rosary beads, simply called a "Rosary" by Catholics, which has a bead for every Hail Mary as well as a dividing bead that separates the five decades one from the other. These prayer beads are dominated by an attached crucifix that signifies the starting point.

All Christians are familiar with the "Our Father," but the "Hail Mary" is a prayer created by merging the words of Gabriel at the time of the Annunciation with the words of Elizabeth to Mary at the time of Mary's visit.

The exact reasons for the great popularity of the Rosary are not really known. It seems to have four elements:

a) the special relationship Mary has with Jesus and her special place in salvation history

b) the opportunity that each mystery affords the faithful to think deeply about a key event in salvation history

c) the repetitive saying ten times of a short prayer, the "Hail Mary," allows a meditative feeling to develop in the mind of the person saying the rosary

d) the tactile feel of beads moving through fingers prayer by prayer calls forth the calming spiritual feeling that mankind has attributed to the handling of beads for several millennium.

The combination of meditation and contemplation together with the touching of beads in one prayer experience is compelling.

Over the years there have been instances where Mary has appeared to people on earth. For instance, in 1531 she appeared to Juan Diego outside of Mexico City asking that a church in her honor be built; this location now has a church dedicated to Our Lady of Guadalupe which attracts more visitors than any other religious location in the Americas. In 1858 she appeared to a 14-year-old girl named Bernadette in southwestern France at Lourdes; this location has attracted thousands who are seeking cures for their ailments; many have been cured as their discarded canes, crutches, and wheelchairs attest. In 1917 she appeared, calling herself the Lady of the Holy Rosary, to three children at Fatima in Portugal. She gave the children predictions and requests regarding the need to pray for the conversion of godless Russia. She predicted the coming of the Second World War.

# The Role of Saints

The Catholic Church has a process called canonization by which certain deceased people's lives are investigated. If they are found to have lived an exemplary life and if miracles are rightly attributed to the deceased person's intercession with God, then the Pope may proclaim that deceased person a saint. Once proclaimed a saint, faithful Catholics are encouraged to pray to the saint asking that they take up specific requests with God in heaven. Since there are nearly 5,000 canonized saints, no individual Catholic is familiar with all of them.

Saints are never adored or prayed to with the expectation that the saint can do anything on their own. Prayers directed to saints are always intercessory in nature. It is true the prayer might thank the saint for the good example they provided the faithful by living a laudatory life or mentioning their particular area of patronage. For instance, the evangelist Luke is the patron of doctors, Thomas More is patron of lawyers, Joan of Arc is the patron of France, the Apostle Jude is the patron of hopeless cases, etc.

# Religious Orders, Catholic Institutions, and the Diocesan Structure

In the brief history included in this short paper, four religious orders are mentioned: the Benedictine, Dominicans, Franciscans, and Jesuits. These four are large and have played a particular historical role in the Church's development but there are several hundred other orders which have been authorized by the Vatican to address other specific needs. These orders have included orders for men, orders for women, and orders for lay people.

Some of the larger traditions, like the Franciscans, have branches that operate with different names but follow the same rule which, in this case, would be the Franciscan Rule or rule of St. Francis of Assisi. There are male Franciscans like the Franciscans of the Eternal Word (that can be seen on the EWTN cable network), the female Franciscans like the Franciscan Sisters of St. Mary (who run several hospitals in the St. Louis area), and there are Third Order groups attached to many Franciscan houses, composed of Catholic laymen and women, that help with the work of the order.

Diocese is a word taken from a Greek word meaning administrative district. The Catholic Church adopted it to describe an area administered by a bishop. Much later the Church began to organize a few dioceses by function. For instance, all priests who serve on US military installations belong to a Catholic military diocese.

In a normal diocese, one that covers a geographic area, the bishop has many functions: assigning priests to parishes, establishing or disestablishing parishes, running diocesan charitable functions, running canon law tribunals that adjudicate such things as requests for annulments, running vocation offices that provide information to young adults who are considering a consecrated life, supporting Catholic educational institutions, arranging for the education of candidates for the diocesan priesthood, arranging financial support for parishes in poorer neighborhoods, providing means of communicating diocesan news to the faithful (e.g., newspapers, magazines, newsletters, letters read at Sunday Mass in the Parishes, etc.), visiting parishes every year or two to administer the sacrament of Confirmation, etc. Additionally a bishop is expected to participate in meetings of the US Conference of Catholic Bishops and serve on other committees as requested by the Vatican.

In a typical Catholic diocese there will be a wide variety of Catholic institutions that perform a wide array of services for the sick, the troubled, the ignorant, and the poor. Some of these institutions are run by religious orders, some by lay groups, and some by the diocese. In the St. Louis area, for instance, Catholics have established four universities, about a dozen high schools, around 100 grade schools, seven hospitals, over a dozen nursing homes, several homeless shelters, etc.

There are in St. Louis representative groups from over two dozen religious orders that range from Discalced Carmelites who spend their lives in contemplative prayer offering the public a quiet chapel to visit and pray quietly with the nuns who are sequestered behind a curtain, to the Benedictines who run a high school and pray as a group several times daily raising their voices in a prayerful chant to God almighty, to Mother Teresa's Missionary Sisters from Calcutta who run a house from which six nuns serve the poorest of the poor in St. Louis' inner city, to a lay group, called Birthright, which advertises and urges girls and women with difficult pregnancies to call for help and financial support so the child might be brought to term and perhaps placed in an adoptive home.

# The Catholic Teaching on Purgatory

The Catholic Church, unlike most Protestant Churches, teaches that there is a place, or a state of being, for the souls of deceased people who have died without having performed adequate penance for their earthly sins. This place is called purgatory and it is a place of both deprivation and anticipation. Deprivation because the soul is unable to be in the presence of God enjoying the intense joy of that heavenly state. Anticipation because the soul realizes that in the future, at some point, their time of purgation shall end, and they shall be admitted to heaven.

The Church teaches that certain holy people have experienced so much suffering on earth that they are immediately admitted to heaven. For example, John Paul II suffered a long illness before his death. This lengthy period of suffering combined with his exemplary life caused him to be declared a saint within a few years of his death.

The Biblical support for this teaching is found in 2 Maccabees (28:43-46) which urges people to say prayers for their deceased friends and relatives asking God to have mercy on their souls. There would be no purpose for such prayers of petition to God if the fate of these souls was totally settled. (It should be noted that Maccabees is not found in many Protestant Bibles.)

# The Catholic View of Grace

Catholics believe there are two kinds of grace: actual grace and sanctifying grace. Sanctifying grace flows to anyone who worthily receives one of the seven sacraments. Actual grace goes to any baptized Christian who prays, or otherwise raises his heart and mind to God and who is free from any unforgiven mortal sin(s).

Going further, Catholics believe there is no salvation for a person who dies with an unconfessed, unforgiven mortal sin. Normally a mortal sin is forgiven through the reception of the sacrament of Reconciliation. In an emergency a mortal sin can be forgiven by the recitation of a perfect act of contrition which is a statement of sorrow for personal sin(s) because such sin is offensive to God who is all good and deserving of all our love.

# The Catholic View of Faith and Good Works

Catholics believe that faith in God, the Father, the Son, and the Holy Spirt, is necessary for salvation. Further, Catholics believe that faith in God can't be arrived at through human effort alone. God's grace and help is necessary for a man to come to belief in God.

For Catholics, good works are an outward sign that God's grace is active in the believer. In other words, while good works are not needed for salvation, their presence is a good outward sign of an inner reality.

At the time of the Reformation some Catholic leaders held that good works were necessary for salvation. This position has been changed to a teaching that good works, while not needed for salvation, are useful for helping our fellow man in this life and also for reducing the punishment for sin that the believer will have to endure in Purgatory during the next life.

# Cardinals, Monsignors, and Other Catholic Titles

In the Catholic Church there are over a dozen titles. Some are honorific, some designate a temporary transitional status, and others a permanent, or long-term appointment. Cardinal and Monsignor are basically honorific titles. There are sometimes special, occasional duties to be performed by these. For instance, Cardinals are called upon to elect a new Pope when the office falls vacant. The addition of the prefix "arch" to the word "bishop" is essentially honorific as well. While bishops have real duties, archbishops are simply bishops performing the same duties in a more populous place.

There are a welter of titles that are temporary or transitional. Usher, acolyte, or lector are names given to a lay Catholic who is performing certain duties at Mass. Titles, such as sub-deacon or transitional deacon, are given to seminarians as they approach their time of ordination. In religious orders titles, such as novice or scholastic, are used for members in transition to final vows or ordination. Finally, there are titles, such as brother, which can be transitional or permanent.

Of course there are a few titles that designate permanent positions with important regular duties. Parish priests run parishes, bishops run dioceses, and of course, the Pope runs the whole church. Since Vatican II, parish priests have been assisted in their duties by permanent deacons who assist at Mass, help priests run parishes, perform Baptisms, witness Marriages, and deliver communion at Mass (or to sick parishioners at their homes.)

# Unique Catholic Practices and Sacramentals

Catholics over the last two millennia have developed a wide array of practices and physical things that remind Catholics of their ever present relationship with and need for God.

To mention a few practices:

a) making the sign of the cross
b) morning and evening prayers
c) grace before a meal
d) genuflecting upon entering a Church
e) developing the habit of saying a short prayer, called an ejaculation, several times a day (examples might include "Lord have mercy on me, a sinner" or "All for the greater honor and glory of God," etc.)

All these are done to focus the mind on God.

To mention a few physical sacramentals (i.e., physical things that call God to mind):

a) taking up some Rosary beads and saying the prayers
b) blessing oneself by taking holy water (i.e., water that has been blessed by a priest) on the tips of the fingers before making the sign of the cross

c) hanging crucifixes or crosses on the walls in the home or placing a statute of Jesus or one of saints on a table top.

In these examples, the sacramentals involved are the Rosary beads, the holy water, and the various statues or items on walls. Sacramentals are often blessed by a priest just before they are placed into service. Once blessed a Sacramental may be given—but not sold—to someone else.

# PART II – THE CHURCH SINCE VATICAN II

# Before Vatican II

Before Vatican II, the Catholic Church was doing a fairly good job of fulfilling the call of its creator, Jesus Christ, to "feed my flock" and to "go forth and convert." More particularly:

a) It was presenting an integrated, complex set of doctrines regarding faith and morals that explained to the faithful where they came from, where they might be going (heaven or hell), how to lead a virtuous life, and how to deal with their sins and failures.

b) It was offering a Latin based mystical and magisterial set of devotions and sacraments, particularly the Mass, that engaged most people in an uplifting, traditional way.

c) The Church was able to staff its churches and schools with enough priests and nuns to provide for a lot of one-on-one engagement with Catholics, particularly the young. This allowed the faithful to gain a fulsome understanding of the Gospels and of the intricacies of the many Church doctrines that grew out of a close analysis of the Gospels. This group was also able to lead the faithful in the practice of its many devotions, rituals, and Sacraments.

In summary, a social scientist (e.g., a cultural anthropologist) might say the Catholic Church was doing a good job—not a perfect job—of:

a) setting forth an integrated set of doctrines
b) providing ceremonies and practices that fit with those doctrines
c) offering the faithful a clerical class of adequate size to convey the doctrines and encourage the faithful to remain strongly involved.

# The Vatican II Period with
# John XXIII and Paul VI

In 1958, Pius XII, a former Vatican diplomat who had seen the Church through WWII, passed away and the Cardinal Archbishop of Venice, Angelo Giuseppe Roncalli, became the new Pope and took the name John XXIII. He had grown up in very modest circumstances but was blessed with a deep faith, a pleasant open personality, and a good mind. Pope John, being one of 13 children and a former soldier, said the Church's rituals and pastoral approaches had not been looked at since the Council of Trent (1545-63). He used the term "Aggiornamento", which means to bring up to date or "freshening up," to describe his goal for the Church.

He decided to call a Council of the Church (Vatican II), and he appointed the conservative Archbishop Marcel-François Lefebvre to organize its agenda. Archbishop LeFebvre, a Holy Ghost Father, had been stationed in Africa as a bishop and had overseen the Church's very successful missionary effort there.

The Council assembled in October 1962 with perhaps 3,000 bishops, their advisers, and observers from other faiths present. Once organized, the Council rejected the limited LeFebvre agenda, deciding instead on a more wide-ranging scope. According to Church tradition, once assembled a Council of the Church is in charge of the Church, that is why in four centuries Popes had called only one Council (Vatican I) which had ended abruptly when the Franco Prussian War erupted.

During Vatican II, Pope John died and a new Pope Paul VI was elected. Additionally, during this period the birth control pill came on the market. Pope Paul decided not to expand the scope of the Council's deliberations to decide the morality of this product; instead he made that decision himself and issued Humanae Vitae on July 25, 1968, which condemned use of "the pill" because it interfered with God's desire to keep each marital act open to conception.

The Council ended on December 8, 1965. Four major documents, three declarations, and nine decrees were issued. Most important for normal Catholics, the Council permitted the Mass to be celebrated in the vernacular, meaning using the common language of the people attending the Mass. Immediately the various bishops moved to implement something called the "spirit of Vatican II." This meant for most Catholics the traditional Latin Masses disappeared quickly and were replaced with Masses in their local language(s). These new liturgies were composed in a rush by local bishops or even parish priests. Many were not faithful to the rules about which liturgical elements needed to be included in a Mass. Most statues were removed from Catholic Churches. The music used at Mass was "updated" just as quickly. Guitars and tambourines replaced organs in many churches. Many felt these Masses had lost any semblance of their historic mystery and majesty. However, the use of local languages did give the people a more direct understanding of the words being used. They no longer had to depend upon the translations set out in the pews.

Most religious orders of nuns adopted more open

lifestyles (e.g., living outside of convents in apartments, wearing habits that could easily be mistaken for business suits, etc.). Many nuns, particularly those with useful training and credentials (e.g., in teaching, social work, or nursing) actually chose to leave their orders. These manifestations of the "spirit of Vatican II" were particularly hard on the Catholic grade schools all across the United States, which were forced to hire lay teachers. Tuitions rose and many schools closed.

Vatican II also removed the Church's former statement that "for those aware of the Catholic Church" there was no salvation outside the Church. This provision had for centuries sent a message to non-Catholics that the Catholic Church thought they were hopelessly lost. The wording in Vatican II was much more welcoming to non-Catholics by simply saying there was much good and truth in these churches and the sincere following of their beliefs could lead to salvation. This opened the door for the many ecumenical discussions that have occurred over the last 50 years. In fact a Lutheran-Catholic discussion in Sweden actually decided there were not doctrinal differences between the two Churches on what was needed to gain salvation.

The implementation of these liturgical changes caused traditionalist Catholics to react negatively. One of those reacting was Archbishop Marcel Lefebvre, who created a new order or movement called the Society of St. Pius X. His priests pledged to retain their exclusive attachment to the Latin Mass. Several years later, he consecrated four new bishops so the society could survive his death. The reason his departure was not a complete rupture with the papacy was his insistence that his group rigorously follow all the sacramental procedures that were in force prior to Vatican II. Since Vatican II had not outlawed or banned these older practices, he was still following acceptable Church rubrics. Of course, his ordaining four priests as bishops was a violation of a Church rule that required the Vatican's specific advanced approval of the consecration of any bishop. This led to the excommunication of Lefebvre and the four new bishops. (Later Pope Benedict XVI lifted these excommunications.)

These changes caused discord in most parishes. With the traditionalists arguing with the reformists in every parish around the world, young people who might be drawn to a religious vocation as a nun or priest began to have second thoughts. Young people attracted to a life of such commitment are generally seeking a stable environment in which to serve others. Vocations began to fall. Seminaries started to close. Orders of nursing and teaching nuns felt the greatest declines. The exceptions were the traditionalist groups: the Society of St. Pius X, other priestly groups that remained traditional, cloistered Carmelites, and other groups of nuns that simply retained their traditional habits. All these held their own or actually gained recruits.

The situation was so desperate that a few years after Vatican II closed, Paul VI said in a homily in November 1972 that "the smoke of Satan" had been let loose inside the Church. Exactly what he was referring to is unclear. Was it the widespread abuse of the liturgy? Was it the discord that arose within most parish communities? Was it the creation of traditionalist groups like the Society of Pius X? Perhaps it was all of these.

When Marcel Lefebvre died, he had three seminaries operating at full capacity: one in the Argentina, one in the U.S., and one in Switzerland. Today the Society operates worldwide with 650 priests, 442 congregations, and has increased its number of seminaries to six. Its country of greatest penetration is France and half of its seminaries are in Europe.

# The John Paul II and Benedict XVI Period

However, all was not lost. After John Paul I, Pope Paul's successor, died after only a month in office, the Cardinals elected John Paul II who was to serve for 26 years until 2005. His gregarious personality, his opposition to Communism, including its Catholic manifestation called "liberation theology," his decision to issue a completely new updated Catechism, his strong support for traditional marriage, and his globe-trotting habits kept the Catholic public enthralled.

All this occurred while his right-hand man, Cardinal Ratzinger, who later followed John Paul II as Benedict XVI, began to bring order out of the chaos that had erupted after Vatican II. The Vatican reasserted strict control over all Mass liturgies used in all languages. The Vatican began looking at all seminary curriculums and faculties to make certain they were orthodox; many changes had to be made. Homosexuality had gotten into several seminaries as standards had been reduced to get more recruits; these seminaries experienced Vatican initiated "house cleanings." The music used at Mass was subjected to limitations—it had to be theologically sound and uplifting, not jarring. There was strong encouragement to use old Latin hymns and to reinsert Latin Prayers (e.g., the Creed or the Our Father) into the liturgy. Theologians who had pushed the envelope on innovations were reined in. The Vatican reasserted its control over the orthodoxy of the faculty at schools calling themselves Catholic. Several Jesuit schools dropped the word Catholic from their literature rather than insist on such orthodoxy from their faculties.

Then John Paul II, with his successor Benedict XVI, actually managed to stabilize the number of vocations. They quieted the traditionalists within the parishes, who for the most part made their peace with the reforms once the flow of changes stopped and a new liturgical status quo settled in. The attendance in the pews in Western Europe and North America stabilized at roughly 50% of the pre-Vatican II attendance. In Latin America there was a continuing slow exodus to Pentecostal Faiths. In Africa, a surge of converts began to send the number of Catholics worldwide up dramatically.

One scandal really rocked the John Paul II papacy. There was a highly successful conservative order called the Legionnaires of Christ founded in the 1940's by Marcial Maciel, a Mexican priest. This order attracted many young men and was expanding into many countries. However, it turned out Maciel was an active bi-sexual. He had fathered children out of wedlock. He was using his position to demand homosexual favors, and then demanding silence, from his abused subordinates in the order. When the scandal came out, the Vatican cashiered Maciel (January 2005) and considered forcing the dissolution of the Legionnaires. In the end, the Legionnaires, after Vatican investigations, were allowed to continue to do their work in 21 countries with their 600 priests.

The number of Catholics in Europe is now roughly equal to the number in Africa, but the European number is shrinking as birth rates fall and atheism gains adherents. The numbers in Africa are growing as people there wish to move away from tribal religions, move toward things western, and want more unity to resist the violence of the encroaching Muslims.

# The Pope Francis I Period

In March 2013 the Cardinals chose Jorge Bregoglio to replace Benedict when he decided to retire. Bregoglio was selected because the Church needed someone to clean up the Vatican bureaucracy which had frustrated Benedict's attempts to clean house, particularly at the Vatican Bank, which had been implicated in money laundering. Bregoglio had a reputation for dealing with difficult Church administrative situations in a country known for its corruption. The new Pope took the name Frances I. He did prove he had the chops to remove powerful members of the Curia (e.g., he pushed Cardinal Raymond Burke out of not one, but two, important positions.)

However, the new Pope Francis showed early on that his principal interest was revising Church teaching on some key moral questions. Since the items he was interested in changing were actually in the New Testament, not in the Church's tradition as the Latin Mass had been, he had to proceed carefully.

He began calling synods of bishops to discuss subjects like "communion for divorced and civilly remarried Catholics." He then carefully stacked the synod's membership with bishops who were interested in change in this area. Later he had an articulate bishop and scholar, who shared the Pope's views, give an address to some assembled Cardinals and bishops. This strategy broke the ice in his preferred areas of "reform." Sometimes he gave an interview to a certain elderly reporter known for his flexible reporting techniques. Francis would then refuse to issue clarifications when his alarming viewpoints hit the newspaper. People did not know whether to attribute the news item to Francis or the elderly reporter's failures. Finally he has issued an Encyclical which has footnotes authorizing local control on this controversial subject.

So far, Pope Francis has managed to put four or five doctrinal "adjustments" on the table that contradict explicit teachings of the New Testament. His moral reforms deal with the sexual morality area which is the same area that mainline Protestant reformers have focused on in the past. Francis supporters feel he is trying to get back the many Catholics who stopped coming to Church because the Church's teachings are too "hard." They also feel he wants to turn more control of these sensitive issues to local pastors and/or diocesan authorities.

In Argentina, Pope Francis had served as provincial of the Jesuits in the 1990's. His administration created discord within that group. Some loved him, while others could barely talk to him. When he was finally replaced, the new provincial had him live in a small house away from other Jesuits. One Argentinian Jesuit was quoted as saying it took 10 to 20 years for the Jesuits in Argentina to come back together after Bregoglio's administration.

Luckily, during his time as provincial he had grown close to the Archbishop of Buenos Aries, Antonio Quarracino, who pulled him from his Jesuit exile to become Auxiliary Bishop. Later Bregoglio became Quarracino's successor.

The difficulty with Pope Francis' approach is that no one has figured out how to maintain unity in a religious congregation that has promulgated conflicting standards for beliefs (doctrines), behavior (morals), and rituals (Mass, etc.). The result has always been a splintering. Vatican II allowed, but did not mandate, a new Mass. Fortunately for unity, essentially the whole Church accepted the new Mass once it was standardized and became familiar.

Although there is a lack of real clarity on his intentions, Francis seems to want to allow local options on changes to church teaching and practice on such things as:

a) communion for the divorced and remarried
b) communion for active homosexuals
c) teaching on the existence of hell
d) teaching on the meaning of "life everlasting", etc.

If essentially the whole Church buys into all these "suggestions," the Church might again dodge a bullet.

The Vatican II liturgical changes were widely adopted. The mainline Catholic churches only lost about 5% of the faithful to openly traditionalist groups. If Francis' changes gain universal or wide acceptance, thus neutralizing the need for the actual implementation of the local control, he will probably retain a high degree of Church unity. In other words, if Francis' changes only cause another 5% to leave, he will have retained a Church of roughly its current size.

Of course, there are two huge "ifs." The first "if" is problematic because there are wide differences in feelings about sexuality across the Church. For instance, Germans seems very welcoming to Francis' changes while the Africans are not at all. The second "if" is also problematic. Whereas Vatican II dealt with changing ritual practices (e.g., the form of the Mass) that were developed by Church leaders between the 6th and 16th centuries, the doctrines Francis currently wants to change come from Jesus himself.

Commentators have noted that such changes have not saved the mainstream Protestant Churches which have had attendance problems following similar doctrinal and jurisdictional changes they made 20 and 30 years ago. These commentators also point out that the strongest parts of the Catholic Church (e.g., across Africa and in traditionalist communities elsewhere) are overwhelmingly conservative, traditionalist supporters of the old Latin Mass, etc. Commentators also point out that the traditionalists are finding it much easier to fill their seminaries and novitiates with devout, highly motivated students.

It seems liberal Catholics will tell a pollster they support any liberalizing move by the Church, but that does not seem to translate into their steady attendance on Sunday. Whereas, traditionalists keep coming to Church even when they grumble about the latest liturgical change or doctrinal innovation.

As certain Church leaders see the world constantly "modernizing" and as they long to "make" the Church relevant to that world, they seem to forget Jesus wanted His disciples to reach out and bring the world His message... not the reverse.

# Recent Issues and Questions

There are a number of Catholic practices and teachings that have drawn significant comment in the news. These include the requirement of priestly celibacy, the condemnation of abortion, the teaching against artificial birth control, and the insistence that marriage be between one man and one woman.

Priestly celibacy only became a firm requirement in the Western Church after the split in 1054 with the Eastern Church. This requirement was formally instituted at the Second Lateran Council of 1139. The Eastern Orthodox have retained the system that existed in earlier times. Under this system the normal parish priest is allowed to be married provided he is married at the time of his ordination. However, order priests like monks and bishops must be unmarried. Under this system most orthodox people interact with a married clergy; however, most of the bishops are selected from the ranks of the order priests and monks. In the 17th and 18th centuries many bishops in the Orthodox world decided to join the Roman Church. They joined on the provision that they retain their liturgy and practice of having married parish priests. Rome agreed so there has been a married priesthood loyal to Rome for centuries.

Additionally, certain married ministers from Protestant Churches have become priests at Catholic parishes and, of course, remained married. Additionally, several entire Anglican churches, following the ordination of women priests in the Anglican Communion, have asked the Vatican to transfer as congregations to Rome. Benedict XVI accommodated these groups by creating an ordinariate which has its own liturgy (a slightly re-written version of the traditional Anglican liturgy), its own rules regarding priestly celibacy, its own bishop (like the military diocese mentioned above), etc. This ordinariate will be another source of married priests, particularly in English-speaking countries.

All the forgoing tends to lead to the conclusion that priestly celibacy, at least at the parish level, will gradually disappear. This should gradually increase the number of married priests in parishes; and it should reduce the number of abuse cases, while increasing the overall number of qualified candidates for seminary training. In fairness it must be acknowledged that the additional cost associated with supporting both a priest and his family will be an additional burden.

However, it should be noted that priestly celibacy remains the norm for most of the Roman Church and this is not likely to officially change anytime soon.

On issues involving marriage and sexuality the Church depends on Natural Law analysis and a close reading of Christ's words. Here the Church looks to the design God gave human beings. If God wanted one man and one woman acting together with Him to create new human life, then that creative act should be protected by the marriage vow just as a new human life thus created should be protected from abortion or infanticide. From this logic it is easy to see why the Church opposes artificial birth control. Such drugs or devices block the possibility of God acting with the couple to create new life. Also it is easy to see why the term "marriage" would be totally inappropriate for homosexual unions because such unions are unnatural and against the Natural Law and because such unions give God no opportunity to work with the couple to create new life. This logic extends easily to a logical condemnation of "test tube" babies and sperm banks.

Divorce and remarriage are very common today. However, the Catholic Church remains committed to the indissolubility of marriage because of the Natural Law which argues for the creation of the family unit that protects and nurtures child development, and because Christ's teachings indicate that marriages should be permanent and free from adultery. The Church realizes that marital separation is, on occasion, justified because of such things as alcoholism, financial irresponsibility, abuse, etc. But the Church does not equate legal separation with a right to remarry.

The Church teaches that a first marriage must be declared a nullity, because of some impediment at the time of the marriage, before a new marriage is allowed. An annulment proceeding requires a formal church hearing with a person appointed by the bishop to investigate and present material to the tribunal supporting the validity of the marriage. Although annulments are more common today than they were in the time of Henry VIII, many annulment petitions are not granted. A legally separated Catholic has not committed a sin and is therefore still eligible to receive communion at Mass. However, a Catholic who is divorced and remarried is living in a state of sin, his life situation indicates he is not attempting to reform his life, and he is not eligible to receive communion.

In recent decades, many priests have been accused of sexual abuse of minors in their congregations. The biggest problem was priests abusing teen-aged boys. It turned out about 2% of priests engaged in this behavior, but about 90% of bishops engaged in helping to cover up the behavior.

Additionally it is interesting that the 2% occurrence rate is more or less in line with the percentage found in other studies of the behavior of adult men who have access to teen-aged boys. The difference with these priests was the amount of media attention given to priest abuse as opposed to the media attention given to the general societal problem of the sexual abuse of teens. Of course, all child abuse is bad and needs to be condemned.

However, in the case of these priest abusers, the bishops generally decided to cover up the abuse by settling the cases and transferring the offending priest to new, unsuspecting parishes. The problems of course compounded themselves until the Vatican under John Paul II and Benedict cracked down and insisted that wrong-doers be drummed out, not transferred. Once the public got wind of the money settlements that had been paid, there was a jump in the number of false claims against priests. There were a few priests who insisted on challenging these false claims, but because of the high cost of litigation most of these priests were not able to pursue litigation.

In any event, this whole sexual abuse scandal meant a reduced number of priests to assign to parishes as the number of young men entering the seminaries was dropping as well for other reasons. One can understand why the bishops engaged in various cover-ups, even as they were unfortunately laying the seeds for the future bankruptcy of several dioceses across the US. As of 2018, the priest abuse scandal has been contained and the number of cases is down, but because of the sinful nature of people, even priests, the problem will never go away completely.

# PART III – THOUGHTS ON MORALITY

# The Catholic Teaching on War

The Catholic Catechism discusses war. This chapter will attempt to apply the Catholic just-war theory to a few examples of war from American history.

Five critical points about going to war and conducting war need to be considered:

a) The acts of the aggressor must have lasting, grave, and certain consequences to the other side.

b) All other means of solving the grievance have been tried and have proved ineffective.

c) There must be serious prospect of success.

d) The war must not produce more pain and disorder than the immediate evil being eliminated.

e) Civilians, their homes, and cities must not be destroyed indiscriminately.

The four wars taken from American history are the Civil War, the Second World War, the Cold War (as though it had turned "hot") and the Iraq War.

# The Civil War

Was the attack by the South on Fort Sumter and/or the South's secession going to have a major, long-lasting, damaging effect on the North? Were protracted discussions with the southern leaders tried in an attempt to limit or end hostilities? Did the North have a serious prospect of success? Was the evil created by the preservation of the Union at the expense of States Rights too great, and could the evil of slavery be eliminated in a less bloody way? Were civilians killed, were their homes and lands razed leaving them susceptible to starvation and disease? Each American has their own judgment, but it looks like the Civil War gets four "no's" and one "yes," that being on the prospect of success by the North.

# World War II

Were the Axis Powers a grave, serious, lasting threat to the Allies? Were negotiations pursued fully or was the "bulldog" Churchill unable to negotiate? Perhaps millions of Jews might have been spared? Were there prospects for success? Was the war likely to produce more or greater evils than it would solve? Was the war conducted with an eye to keeping civilian casualties and destruction of cities to a minimum? Here the consensus would probably be three yes's and two no's. The two no's being the "producing greater evil" point and the "failure to protect civilians and their property." Remember the repression of eastern Europe under the USSR that followed VE day, and the wholesale destruction of Axis cities by the Allied bombers.

# The Cold War (As If It Had Turned Hot)

This war never really became a fighting war. The two sides essentially blustered and negotiated for so long that one society finally changed and the great hostility subsided. But if it had become a hot war by the USSR attacking the US, these would have been the considerations. Was the USSR a grave threat to the US? Were negotiations exhausted? Was there a serious prospect of the US succeeding? Would a greater evil have ensued if there had been a nuclear exchange? Would civilians have been unduly affected?

Here there are three yes's and two no's, but the two no's are unthinkable. Massive destruction of civilians and cities in both countries, and of course, the likely destruction of all human life from fallout.

# The Iraq War

Was the "coalition of the willing" really gravely threatened by Iraq? Had all other means such as the embargo and overflights exhausted their usefulness? Was there a prospect of taking Bagdad and capturing Saddam? Was a greater evil likely to emerge, such as sectarian violence and ethnic cleansing of neighborhoods? Were civilians unduly affected, considering that only ten percent of the population have been displaced and about 50,000 have been killed? Here there is one yes and four no's. The single yes was the US's likely ability to take Bagdad and capture Saddam.

Setting the Cold War aside because it never became a "hot" war, the US comes off poorly as these five measures are applied to these three war situations. There are five yes's when the Catholic Church would require fifteen yes's to go forward. The weakest showings were the Civil War and the Iraq war. The best showing was WWII. But none made it to the acceptable threshold.

The actual handling of the Cold War is the best example of how to handle serious international conflicts. This chapter must acknowledge this great American success.

In the area of "hot" wars actually fought that were just, the Korean War is probably the best example. It is possible that this war would get five yes's if subjected to the analysis used above.

# The Option to Sin

On St. Valentine's Day, the nation always turns to thoughts of love. The word love is so overused and yet so important. Great acts of love come to mind. The soldier who saves his friends by falling on a live grenade, the parents who lovingly and with no complaint care for their polio-paralyzed son, the nun in Calcutta who tends to the dying as they are brought in from the streets outside, etc. But there are even greater acts of love.

Think of God's great love for man. He created a great universe for man to inhabit with time, space, plants, animals, a solar system, DNA, and myriad other things; all for man to investigate, explore and turn to his own uses. He seems to have done this in various ways using such things as "divinely directed evolution" for some things, great explosions for other things, and miraculous infusions of special characteristics for still others. For instance, when it was time for man to be separated from the animal kingdom, God evidently did this by the infusion of a soul along with self-awareness and awareness of God. He created man with both a conscience and free will so each man might know the difference between "good" and "evil" and might further decide for himself whether to do good or evil. God loved each of these humans and he wanted each of them to respond by seeking God and doing good. Of course, there was a wholesale rejection of the good and even a pronounced preference for the evil, so God turned again to love to guide men back.

This time God sent Jesus to perform this second great act of love both for mankind, in general, and for each man, in particular. This man, Jesus, was/is said to be the Son of God by Christians, and just a particularly good man by most Jews and Muslims. Regardless, Jesus came to do two things: He explained to man that God loves all men and that it was important to do good by loving God and helping other people; and He suffered and died explicitly as an expiation for all the evil and sin that man had done (and continues to do) in this world. Jesus's gruesome death is recorded in the histories of the time and serves as a perpetual reminder of God's great love for man.

Neither of these acts of love have left the world without both physical and moral evil. Sickness besets man, hurricanes still destroy cities, bad men continue to rob, pillage, and commit abortions, and all men on occasion find themselves falling short or—put more bluntly—sinning. However, now God has given man a way to deal with all this.

Regarding suffering, just as Jesus answered God's call and took up his cross, men who are suffering are urged to offer their individual crosses up as smaller acts of love, to join with and participate in Jesus's great act of love and suffering on His cross in Palestine 2000 years ago.

For those who have sinned, God urges them to ask forgiveness claiming part of the infinite supply of love and grace that Jesus earned by voluntarily dying on that cross 2000 years ago. (For Catholic and Orthodox Christians, the forgiveness comes explicitly through the sacrament of Reconciliation where a formal recitation of sins is followed by a formal statement of sorrow for those sins, followed further by forgiveness of those sins being dispensed by an ordained priest who is acting in God's place for the occasion. For other Christians, and those of other religions who hold Jesus in high regard, forgiveness is obtained by fervently praying that the sin in question be forgiven by God and that God provide special grace so sin might be avoided in the future.)

And so when St. Valentine's Day rolls around, it is good to think of these two great acts of love by God and Jesus for the benefit of each man.

# Magisterium vs. Conscience

The Church has a wonderful magisterium that explains how scriptures, natural law, and tradition all mesh together to give Catholics an integrated belief structure for dealing with questions of faith and morals. But church leaders have to be prepared to speak clearly and quickly when important moral teachings are challenged or undermined. If they don't, these Church leaders are not living up to their duty and could actually commit sins of omission.

The magisterium is the authentic, authoritative teaching of the Church. The good Catholic must submit his mind and will to this teaching, whether said teaching has been promulgated by a council of the Church or by a Papal pronouncement, such as an "ex cathedra" statement or more commonly as an encyclical.

For normal Catholics, such authoritative teachings are to be found in:

    a)   the words of the liturgy
    b)   the letters of local bishops read at Sunday Mass
    c)   articles by the local bishop published in various newspapers
    d)   the instruction given at Confession

e)   the homilies delivered at Mass.

For more studious Catholics there is always the option of reading Canon Law, the Catechism, or the documents, statements, and encyclicals themselves.

Today there is a great debate in the Church about how far the practicing Catholic must go in submitting to the magisterium of the Church. In other words, when may the Catholic begin to follow his conscience?

This issue is more hotly debated today because civil leaders, judges, and law-makers in Western Europe and North America repeatedly opt to give people freedoms and/or legal courses of action which the Church holds are immoral. In the middle ages the civil law and Church law tended to line up with each other, in other words that which was immoral was also illegal. With the coming of the enlightenment, some immoral items were dropped from the civil law, but everyone continued to understand that these were still immoral.

Today large organized groups actually push to have immoral things approved in law such that all society, including Catholics, must acquiesce or even participate in immorality. The youth, including Catholic youth, become confused and are pushed to conform to the fashion of the day. Many buy into one or more of the new fashions. They reject the teaching of the Church, but because of family tradition they want to remain in the Catholic Church. They then begin to look for ways to invoke the "right of conscience" to selectively override certain parts of the magisterium.

This discussion has been rather theoretical. None of the most troubling governmental departures have been mentioned. Perhaps a short list would serve to refresh everyone's recollection of the hottest of these hot issues: legalization of abortion; government funding of abortion; declaring a preemptive war; funding of preemptive war; participation in preemptive war; stem cell research; legalizing gay marriage; legalizing birth control pills; failing to adequately provide for the poor; authorizing the wholesale transfer of jobs overseas; etc. Some of these are clearly condemned by the magisterium of the Church; with others it is less clear.

Obviously legalizing abortion and government funding of abortion are clear violations and Archbishop Burke has said so in no uncertain terms, and placed restrictions on pro-abortion Catholics who want to receive communion. One is thankful for Burke's action but one also asks where were Carberry, May, and Rigali on these restrictions on communion?

A less clear situation is a government policy that authorizes and encourages the movement of 340,000 manufacturing jobs out of Ohio. Obviously the Church has spoken about the need for society to promote job creation so men can support their families, but it's not clear that employing 340,000 Chinese instead of 340,000 Ohioans is not acceptable morally. Would a State Department official, who happened to be a Catholic, be committing a sin if he helped arrange for the loss of 340,000 jobs in Ohio? Would his act be mitigated if he could say, "But I also arranged for the Chinese to hire 1,000 lawyers and accountants at high salaries in New York to do their paperwork for the importation of the manufactured goods that the 340,000 Chinese will make in China for shipment back into Ohio for sale at Wal-Mart?"

While the Church has spoken clearly on abortion, the Church's teaching on other issues is less than clear and leaves wiggle room, in other words it leaves room for an individual's conscience. Preemptive war in Iraq was a recent example. The Church's negative teaching on preemptive war through history is clear. However, when the US was getting ready for such a war, the Church did not issue a letter to all American Catholics saying that participation or support for the war would be sinful. In theory, that would have changed the entire complexion of things for all Catholics and perhaps many Protestants as well. Instead, the Church left the situation in a state of flux. Well-informed Catholics knew a violation of the Church's injunction against preemptive war was about to occur. These Catholics saw the Pope's envoy come to America and discuss the issue with President Bush. But the Pope never spoke publicly to Catholics on the issue.

# Does God's Plan Require that Evil and Suffering be Part of Human Life?

Evil exists in the world created by an all-perfect God. How can God allow evil to exist when, after all, he is all-good?

Before focusing on evil, it probably makes more sense to consider God's overall plan for man. God has created an intelligent being, man, that can do several important things.

First, man can know that God exists. He can know this through faith and by being exposed to the revealed word of God, but man can also know God exists through his reason and the study of things about him. So man can know God.

Second, God has given each man a basic sense of right behavior and wrong behavior. This is called a conscience. Every man has a conscience, and with education or formation a person's conscience can be refined and brought to a fuller understanding of right and wrong. So man can know what is right behavior and what is wrong behavior.

Third, God has given each man a free will. This free will allows each man as he goes through life to choose the good or choose the bad. So man has the free will to either turn toward God or turn away from God.

Fourth, God has a desire to draw all men to Him. However, He knows that some men will choose the "wrong" rather than the "good" and in so choosing they will be turning away. Again, God wishes to honor this free choice so he allows those that turn away to live their eternity in their preferred way, away from God. So man must be aware that there are real long-term consequences in their choices.

Now the time has come to look more carefully at evil. There are various types of evil in the world and each deserves a little consideration.

First, there is evil caused by man's inhumanity to man. Stalin was a man who arranged to kill about 60 million people. But there is also the handsome cad who dates half a dozen girls, breaks their hearts, and leaves half of them pregnant out of wedlock. There is the student who discovers that his teacher's hearing aid will squeal loudly if exposed to a screeching sound, so he carries an un-oiled screw device and when near that teacher he gives his device a good crank, sending the teacher into auricular pain. Man-on-man evil comes in all sizes, big to small, but it has the common element of one or more people using their free will to inflict pain and suffering on their fellow man. This kind of evil is a perfectly understandable outgrowth of free will improperly used. God could not use his power to stop this kind of evil without taking away some men's free will, and that would be too great an infringement on God's grand plan as set out above.

Second, there is evil that comes from natural causes. Epidemics, aging, accidents, hurricanes, earthquakes, etc., are examples of things that God initiates that cause lots of pain, suffering, and death. Part of God's plan is to draw people to himself for eternity. This means that all men must die. Some die quickly with little suffering, but many die slowly with lots of suffering. Think of the person afflicted with polio or the women dying of a breast cancer that comes and goes over a decade. There are those who lose everything in an earthquake, but are left alive with no resources. Physically healthy—but suffering none the less. These long-term suffering situations cause a lot of people to lose their belief in an all-powerful, all-loving God. They ask why God allows such long-term suffering?

The answer lies in the response "believers" give to such suffering:

First, looking at those enduring suffering: Do they respond by enduring it with joy and offering it up to God as a recompense for the times they (or their fellow humans) chose "the wrong" rather than "the right"? They might learn from great historical figures who have suffered. They think of Jesus of Nazareth, or Joan of Arc, or the Ugandan Martyrs, or Ignatius of Loyola, or Francis of Assisi, or Thomas More. These are people who have endured long-term disability or incarceration leading to execution. They said during their periods of trial, "I stand with my God and although I don't fully understand why I am in this predicament, I accept it as a mystery and even as a gift from God." These people saw their suffering as something to welcome with joy, as something God in his infinite wisdom wanted them to go through. Religious mystics, particularly Christian mystics, speak of suffering as a gift uniting them to God. Christians speak of suffering as a way of participating in and even augmenting the suffering Christ endured on the Cross. In this way, a suffering person can visualize his personal suffering as not only an expiation of his own sin but also as joining with Christ's suffering to overcome the sins of all men. Individual suffering can in this way be seen as a great benefit to all mankind. This logic has penetrated Catholic thought so much that the typical devout Catholic will say, when faced with suffering, "this is my cross." Theologians feel that except for the fall of Adam and Eve, suffering would not exist. However, because of the fall and original sin, man has to endure suffering.

Second, looking at those who are viewing others suffering: What is their response? Do they try to find a way to help others avoid such suffering in the future? Do they comfort the afflicted? Do they oppose the dictator who's torturing people? God puts these terrible situations before them so they might demonstrate their orientation either toward God or away from God.

Having said all this, the one thing that can be said with assurance is that human suffering is certainly a part of God's plan. It remains profoundly true, although man's ability to understand suffering is limited. Some aspects of suffering are intelligible, but other aspects remain a mystery that can only be glimpsed dimly.

# CONCLUSION

This document does not attempt to answer all questions that a non-Catholic Christian might have about the Catholic Church, but hopefully it helps to explain the logic behind much that makes the Catholic Church what it is.

# A Deeper Exploration into Some Early Saints

# St. Jerome's Gift: The Vulgate

St. Jerome is a Doctor of the Church. He was born in 342 AD in the Balkans and died in 420 AD in Bethlehem. He was originally buried in the Church of the Nativity and later his remains were moved to Rome. He now lies somewhere in the Sistine Chapel of the Basilica of Santa Marie Maggiore. Jerome, who was born Eusebius Hieronymous Sophronius, came from an upper-middle class family that provided him with a good education, first at home and later in Rome. He was good with languages, enjoyed translating inscriptions, but was also inclined toward the libertine life. Jerome had an irascible personality that tended to either attract people or repel them. When he was eighteen, he began to move toward the faith of his parents, and he was baptized by the Pope in that year.

Jerome at 21 began to travel and to collect copies of various manuscripts. He visited Gaul and studied for a time back in his home town in the Balkans. At this time in his life he was exposed to the Arian heresy and decided to oppose it. However, eventually he set out for the Middle Eastern desert in search of solitude and proximity to the source of his faith. Jerome attended some religious lectures in Antioch where he met Bishop Apollinaris before going to the desert to study and practice austerity. In the desert Jerome was afflicted with distracting and sinful recollections of his libertine youth in Rome. He felt that his reading of Rome's early authors was the cause of these distracting thoughts, so in this period he swore off any reading of pagan authors. With the help of a Jew who had converted to Christianity, he threw himself into the study of Hebrew, mostly as a distraction from his wayward, sinful thoughts. At age 31, Jerome was ordained a priest in Antioch with the understanding that the Bishop would not give him any assignments.

At age 38, Jerome went to Constantinople to study the scriptures under the Greek Bishop of that city. Two years later he accompanied the Bishop of Antioch to Rome for a Council to study the religious controversies that were raging in Syria at the time. Pope Damasus (now St. Damasus) was so impressed with Jerome he kept him in Rome as his assistant until he died. Jerome was then 42 years old. Damasus's successor was put off by Jerome's personality, so Jerome headed back to the Middle East. This time Jerome settled in Bethlehem and began to focus more intently on the Scriptures. He sought out local scholars to teach him Chaldaic—an ancient language that had been used for the Books of Tobias and Daniel—and to improve his knowledge of Hebrew.

Jerome was now ready for the great work of his life— translating the entire Bible from its original languages into Latin. Before he died at the age of 78 he had translated or refined earlier translations of all books of the bible except Wisdom, Ecclesiasticus, Baruch, and Maccabees. His translation into Latin (known as the Vulgate) served as the source of nearly all knowledge of the Bible in Western Europe for over one thousand years.

However, Jerome did not give up all other work. He helped St. Paula establish a house for religious ladies in

Jerusalem, and he engaged in a wide-ranging correspondence which provides scholars with a good source for understanding life in the 4th century. He was not a deep or creative thinker, but he did have a clear understanding of correct doctrine as well as a mastery of language. This combination of traits made him a particularly effective counterweight to the dissenters and heretics of his era— Arian, Appolinaris, Oriegn, and on one occasion, even the great St. Augustine himself.

St. Jerome's life is a great example of the mystery that is the unfolding of God's plan. Recall that it was St. Jerome's responses to sinful thoughts that caused him to immerse himself in the study of Hebrew. Later it was this study which allowed St. Jerome to do his great work creating the Vulgate. In similar fashion, it was Jerome's irascible personality that didn't sit well with Damasus's successor. This rejection caused Jerome to return to the Holy Land and to take on the major work of his life which brought the Bible to Western Europe. Out of evil comes good; out of suffering comes victory.

# St. Gregory's Gift: Insight into the Mystery of the Trinity

Gregory of Nazianzen (c. 329 – 390), also known as Gregory the Theologian, was a 4th-century Archbishop of Constantinople and theologian. He is widely considered the most accomplished rhetorical stylist of the patristic age. As a classically trained orator and philosopher, he infused Hellenism into the early church, establishing the paradigm of Byzantine theologians and church officials.

Gregory made a significant impact on the shape of Trinitarian theology among both Greek and Latin-speaking theologians, and he is remembered as the "Trinitarian Theologian." Much of his theological work continues to influence modern theologians, especially in regard to the relationship among the three Persons of the Trinity. Along with the brothers Basil the Great and Gregory of Nyssa, he is known as one of the Cappadocian Fathers.

Gregory is a saint in both Eastern and Western Christianity. In the Roman Catholic Church, he is numbered among the Doctors of the Church; in the Eastern Orthodox Church and the Eastern Catholic Churches he is revered as one of the Three Holy Hierarchs, along with Basil the Great and John Chrysostom.

At the time of Gregory there were three types of heresies going around regarding the person and nature of Jesus Christ:

a) The denial of Christ's Divinity—which led to heresies such as Arianism (others include: Ebonism, Arianism (Jehovah's Witnesses), Nestorianism, Socinianism, Liberalism, Humanism, and Unitarianism.)

b) The denial of Christ's two natures—which created heretical groups such as Monophysitism, Eutychianism, and Monothelitism. These all confuse the two natures of Christ (and tend to absorb one of His natures into the other in one way or the other.)

c) The denial of Christ's humanity—which gave rise to heresies such as Apollinarianism, Docetism, Marcionism, Gnosticism, Apollinarianism, Monarchianism, Patripassianism, Sabellianism, Adoptionism, and Dynamic Monarchianism.

All of these heresies in some way ended up by "dividing" the anthropic (God-Man) Jesus Christ.

Gregory is also one of only three men in the life of the Orthodox Church who have been officially designated "Theologian" by epithet, the other two being St. John the Evangelist and St. Symeon.

## Gregory at Constantinople

Following Constantine's edict which allowed the practice of Christianity together with the clear doctrinal pronouncement of the Council of Nicea in 325 AD, Christian orthodoxy began spreading throughout the empire.

However, Julian the Apostate become emperor in 360 and attempted to restore pagan worship across the empire. This submerged Christianity for a time and allowed heresies to recover and even flourish. After Julian died in 363, there were three emperors who accommodated Arian heretics.

The last of these was Valens, who died in 378. The accession of Theodosius I, a steadfast supporter of Nicene orthodoxy, was good news for those who wished to purge Constantinople of the Arian and Apollinarian heresies. The exiled Nicene party gradually returned to the city. In 379, from his deathbed, Basil reminded the other bishops of Gregory's capabilities and likely recommended his friend to champion the Trinitarian cause in Constantinople.

In 379, the Antioch synod and its archbishop, Meletios, asked Gregory to go to Constantinople to lead a theological campaign to win over that city to Nicene orthodoxy. After some hesitation, Gregory agreed. His cousin Theodosia offered him a villa for his residence; Gregory immediately transformed much of it into a church, naming it Anastasia, "a scene for the resurrection of the faith." From this little chapel he delivered powerful discourses on Nicene doctrine, explaining the nature of the Trinity and the unity of the Godhead. Refuting those who denied the Holy Spirit's divinity, Gregory offered this argument:

"Look at these facts: Christ is born, the Holy Spirit is His forerunner. Christ is baptized, the Spirit bears witness to this.

Christ works miracles, the Spirit accompanies them. Christ ascends, the Spirit takes His place. What great things are there in the idea of God which are not in His power? What titles appertaining to God do not apply also to Him, except for Un-begotten and Begotten? I tremble when I think of such an abundance of titles, and how many Names they blaspheme, those who revolt against the Spirit!"

Gregory's homilies were well received and attracted ever-growing crowds to Anastasia. Fearing his popularity, his opponents decided to strike. On the vigil of Easter, an Arian mob burst into his church during worship services, wounding Gregory and killing another bishop. Escaping the mob, Gregory next found himself betrayed by his erstwhile friend, the philosopher Maximus, who was in secret alliance with Peter, bishop of Alexandria. Maximus attempted to seize Gregory's position and have himself ordained bishop of Constantinople. Shocked, Gregory decided to resign his office, but the faction faithful to him induced him to stay and ejected Maximus. However, the episode left him embarrassed and exposed him to criticism as a provincial simpleton unable to cope with the intrigues of the imperial city.

Affairs in Constantinople remained confused as Gregory's position was still unofficial and Arian priests occupied many important churches. The arrival of the emperor Theodosius in 380 settled matters in Gregory's favor. The emperor, determined to eliminate Arianism, expelled the Arian bishop of Constantinople. Gregory was subsequently enthroned as bishop of Constantinople at the Basilica of the Apostles.

## Theological and Other Works

Gregory's most significant theological contributions arose from his defense of the doctrine of the Trinity. He is especially noted for his contributions to the theology concerning the nature of the Holy Spirit. In this regard, Gregory is the first to use the idea of procession to describe the relationship between the Spirit and the Godhead: "The Holy Spirit is truly Spirit, coming forth from the Father indeed but not after the manner of the Son, for it is not by generation but by procession." Gregory further pointed out he used the word procession "since I must coin a word for the sake of clearness." Although Gregory does not fully develop the concept, this idea of procession would shape most later thought about the Holy Spirit.

He emphasized that Jesus did not cease to be God when he became a man, nor did he lose any of his divine attributes when he took on human nature. Furthermore, Gregory asserted that Christ was fully human, including a full human soul. He also proclaimed the eternal existence of the Holy Spirit, saying that the Holy Spirit's actions were somewhat hidden in the Old Testament but much clearer since the ascension of Jesus into Heaven and the descent of the Holy Spirit at the feast of Pentecost.

In contrast to the Neo-Arian belief that the Son is "unlike" the Father, and to the Semi-Arian assertion that the Son is "like" the Father, Gregory and his fellow Cappadocians maintained the Nicaean doctrine of consubstantiality of the Son with the Father. The Cappadocian Fathers asserted that God's nature is unknowable to man; they helped to develop the framework of hypostasis, or three persons united in a single Godhead; illustrated how Jesus is the eikon of the Father; and explained the concept of the-o-sis, the belief that all Christians can be assimilated with God in "imitation of the incarnate Son as the divine model."

Apart from several theological discourses, Gregory was also one of the most important early Christian men of letters and a very accomplished orator, perhaps one of the greatest of his time. Gregory was also a very prolific poet who wrote theological, moral, and biographical poems.

In bad health, St. Gregory lived for six years after retiring as Archbishop of Constantinople. During this period he composed many beautiful poems, including a long poem about his own life.

## Filioque Controversy

Long after Gregory's death, a very consequential event occurred related to the changes urged by Gregory at Constantinople in 381.

In the late 6th century, some Latin-speaking churches added the words "and from the Son" (Filioque) to the description of the procession of the Holy Spirit, in what many Eastern Orthodox Christians have argued is a violation, since the words were not included in the text by either the Council of Nicaea or that of Constantinople, two councils where the entire Church was represented. This Filioque change was fully incorporated into the liturgical practice of Rome in 1014. Filioque eventually became one of the main causes for the East-West Schism in 1054, and has been an ongoing barrier to reunion between Eastern and Western Christianity.

# St. John Chrysostom, the Eucharistic Doctor

St. John Chrysostom was born about 344 and died in 407. His father was a military officer, his mother was very virtuous, and he studied public speaking under a great teacher of that age, Libanius. He suffered from poor health, but was drawn to a life of asceticism in the mountains. However, his health would not allow such a life so he became a priest in the diocese of Antioch. His brilliance and preaching were widely praised. His now famous Mass was first celebrated in Antioch. His renown was so extraordinary that he was actually kidnapped outside of Antioch one day by agents of the Emperor and taken to Constantinople where he became Patriarch. He brought his form of the Mass to his new Cathedral, the Hagia Sophia. He was deeply loved by the average member of his flock; however, he continued to preach against lavish living which put him at odds with other important clerics and those around the imperial court.

St. John kept up a regular correspondence with Rome over the proper way to handle the various schismatic movements around Asia Minor. A working relationship developed between John, the Patriarch, and the Roman Pope which served both well over the years.

St. John was eventually exiled from Constantinople because of his sermons against lavish living. This exile, while originally to rather comfortable quarters, was intensified. At age 63, he was further exiled to a far frontier of the empire. He died in transit to his new place of exile.

## Eucharistic Teachings and Work

St. John's teachings on the Eucharist were shaped by his belief that the worst sin is to receive communion with serious, unconfessed, unforgiven sin on the soul. His preference was that at Mass the faithful should always envision Christ naked and immolated... not nicely-clothed while eating with or talking to friends. He said, "When Mass is being celebrated, the sanctuary is filled with countless angels who adore the divine victim immolated on the altar."

John followed St. Basil, whose Mass was the first standardized Divine Liturgy. St. Basil's liturgy had become the standard liturgical format used in the east once the Church was freed from its persecuted status in AD 315.

The Basil liturgy was rather long, taking about four hours to complete. St. John came along 50 years later and took on the task of paring that liturgy down to a more manageable length. Once St. John's Mass was finalized, the eastern church had a liturgy that took only an hour and a half. This divine liturgy has come down to us today and is known as the Divine Liturgy of St. John Chrysostom. This Mass is used in the eastern church (both Orthodox and Uniate) for about 90% of all liturgies. Although the liturgy of St. Basil is still used in Eastern Churches, it is only used about 30 times a year.

## St. John's Influence in the West

But why is St. John Chrysostom called the Eucharistic Doctor in the west as well as the east? Here it is important to note that St. John was very close to the Bishop of Rome and had advised the Pope on many important issues including:

a) how to handle schismatic groups in Christendom. Here St. John advocated the use of patience and love rather than a heavy-handed approach.

b) how the church should respond when the Emperor, or any civil ruler, imposes exile on a bishop forcing him out of his See. This problem had affected St. John himself who was twice exiled.

c) steady communication on how to best design a doctrinally complete Mass for the Church, both in the Latin west and Greek east, that adequately instilled in the faithful a sense of the enormity of Christ's sacrifice and the profound union that occurs when the worthy believer receives the host.

This chapter is most concerned with the last of these points.

It is almost certain that St. John gave the Pope help on preparing the words to be used in the Canon of the Latin Mass as well as the actions and bodily positioning to be used by the priest to convey both the sacrificial and communal aspects of the Mass. By AD 425, after St. John's death, the Mass in its several approved variations was in the process of being standardized across the Christian world.

The use of lattice screens and iconostasis positioned between the faithful and the priest helped create a sense in the faithful of the infinite mystery and majesty of the liturgy. The repetitive use of the sign of the cross, genuflecting, and the burning incense reinforced these feelings as well.

The positioning of the priest facing away from the

faithful and toward a dominating crucifix tied all present, the clergy and faithful alike, into a feeling of personal sinfulness, gratitude for the sacrificial action of Christ on the cross, and deep gratitude for the opportunity to receive Christ's body in communion.

This standardization of the Mass became very rigid in the west following the Council of Trent (1545 to 1563). This very rigid standardized Mass, called the Tridentian Mass, follows—from the Sanctus to the Communion—almost word for word the Divine Liturgy of St John Chrysosdom which been created 1,100 years earlier.

These standardized features remained in the liturgies in both the east and the west until Vatican II, when the western Church decided to re-focus on a new format designed to generate a sense of community, with the priest speaking the local language and facing the faithful.

This was the western Church's attempt to re-create the feeling that was perhaps present at the Last Supper. While this is laudatory, it loses the sense of mystery and majesty and deep sense of the forgiveness of sin flowing from Christ's sacrifice that Basil, Chrysostom, and earlier Popes felt were important.

Looked at another way, this is perhaps most appropriate for the modern Church because in the twenty-first century people are very scientifically aware and tend to resist anything engendering "mystery and majesty." Additionally, modern men are very psychologically aware, so they are more apt to seek understanding of the causes of misbehavior, rather than simply acknowledge man's sinfulness and the need for grace and forgiveness.

However, the Eastern Orthodox Church and the Uniate Churches have retained their traditional St. John Chrysostom and St. Basil liturgies.

# The Introduction of the New Mass

St. John Chrysostom is the Catholic Doctor of the Eucharist. One might say he is the patron saint or chief designer of the Mass. Today 90% of Masses celebrated in the eastern church follow the Divine Liturgy of St. John Chrysostom. From 1600 to 1970, all the Masses said in the western church followed the wording created for this Divine Liturgy in the sections from the Sanctus to the Communion.

However, the design of the Mass has been a particularly sensitive issue in the western church since Vatican II. Herein lies the seed of a questionable anti-historical trend.

Following Vatican II, the western Catholic church (but not the eastern church) decided to do a wholesale re-design of the Mass, rejecting nearly all the traditional language and ritual practice that had been integral to the western Mass for 1600 years. Many, perhaps most, of these older design features had grown out of the work of St. John Chrysostom done in the late 4th century.

Essentially the Vatican II liturgical experts decided to create a Mass designed to recall the feelings that had been present at the Last Supper. But the traditional Mass as designed in the 4th century, as the Church emerged from its persecuted status, had incorporated both the feelings engendered by the Last Supper as well as the Crucifixion. When Vatican II dropped most of the feelings engendered by the Crucifixion, it fundamentally changed the tone and thrust of the Mass.

Once the New Mass was understood to be a fundamentally different kind of Mass, many local liturgists began to experiment with the wording, ritual practices, and the music. Two Popes—John Paul II and Benedict XVI— worked diligently to correct obvious errors in wording and to declaim against liturgical abuses in music and practices that had sprung up. However, it was impossible to bring the

New Mass back into any kind of alignment with the Traditional Mass.

Supporters of the New Mass have steadfastly maintained that the Vatican II Mass is actually a correction of improper features that had been introduced into the Mass over the centuries. Further, they hold that the New Mass gives the Church at long last a correct Mass. Supporters of the New Mass have gone so far as to induce bishops to positively ban the saying of the Traditional Mass. Fortunately, the recent Popes have ordered that local bishops make the Traditional Mass available in their locales. The response of local bishops has been spotty. Some offer one Traditional Mass per week at a single location in their diocese. Others have been more accommodating.

## Impact of the New Mass on the Reputation of St. John Chrysostom

In the post Vatican II period, some Catholic authors who write about early church leaders have handled St. John's contribution very circumferentially. These authors write him up sometimes at great length with little or no mention of the Mass and yet his title is Eucharist Doctor. They finesse this by leaving out his doctrinal title and then focusing on St. John's lesser statements about the other sacraments, particularly Holy Orders and Matrimony (*Living the Mysteries - A Guide for Unfinished Christians* by Scott Hahn and Mike Aquilina, 2003). Others, who write shorter pieces, simply change his title from Doctor of the Eucharist to Doctor of Sacred Orators. It is true St. John was a great orator, but for 16 centuries his contribution was manifest in the Mass, not public speaking (*Lives of the Saints* by Rev. Hugo Hoever, 1999). Still others who assemble quotations from early fathers intentionally select quotes that bear on all things except the Mass. Through selective use of quotations, such authors can give the impression that St. John was a great Catholic thinker, without touching on his greatest quotes and works which deal with the Mass as a means to recall Christ's death on the Cross (*The ThirtyThree Doctors of the Church* by Rev. Fr. Christopher Rengers O.F.M.Cap., 2000).

In sum, St. John's reputation and great contributions are being reduced, reinterpreted, and changed so that the New Mass might be presented to the average Catholic without a need for any historical context. These New Mass advocates see the Mass as a ritual practice that began on Holy Thursday and then suddenly appeared in modern life essentially unchanged.

## Recommendation to the Church

The Vatican must require that articles and books mentioning St. John Chrysostom which desire a Nihil Obstat or Imprimatur bring out his great contribution of the Church's development of the Mass, in particular, and Christ's sacrifice on Good Friday, more generally. However, it is unlikely to happen.

Today the Church seems to want neither to focus on its 2000-year history nor to emphasize the reality of sin and the need for sacramental grace, repentance and forgiveness. However, St. John's Mass is a huge historical reality and does emphasize the reality of sin and the need for sacramental grace, repentance and forgiveness. This chasm is huge and needs to be addressed.

# St. John Cassian

(Note: Much of this essay comes from a lecture given by Thomas Merton on May 19, 1963 to his fellow monks at Gethsemane Abbey in Kentucky.)

St. John Cassian was born in the late 4th century in what is today Bulgaria. He was well-educated and fluent in both Greek and Latin. He became a monk in an early monastery located near Jerusalem where he was exposed to eastern monasticism. He began to travel in about 390, first to Egypt to study the desert monks in that country, later to Constantinople where he joined the group of advisers around the patriarch St. John Chrysostom. When John Chrysostom was sent into exile by the Emperor for preaching against lavish living, Cassian was one of the clerics who argued before the Emperor to allow Chrysostom to return to Constantinople, but to no avail. He then traveled to Rome to get the Pope to intervene in the matter. Again the Emperor was unmoved. Chrysostom died in exile. Once in the west, John Cassian decided to settle in southern France near Marseille, where he founded the first monastery in western Europe.

Cassian's monastic rule, contained in his works entitled *Institutes & Conferences*, became the model that St. Benedict later used for his new religious order, the Benedictines.

John Cassian became embroiled in the raging conflict with Pelagianism, which taught that a man was able to live a perfect life without the help of God. St. John Cassian wrote eloquently about the back and forth process wherein man uses grace to move slightly toward God and then with additional grace and personal effort he is able to move even further toward God. This process goes back and forth until the man can move into full alignment with God. St. John believed in a process relationship between each man and God, rather than a static relationship. This approach allowed for each man's free will to have sway in the process. Later, St. John's teaching was used to qualify St. Augustine's teaching that all salvation results solely from God's grace. This is the Augustinian teaching that was taken much further by Protestant teachers in later centuries to justify their sole focus on grace to the point of teaching predestination and even rejecting the existence of man's free will.

However, in his lecture Merton was not so interested in Cassian on grace; instead focusing on Cassian's teachings on prayer.

Cassian argues that a person prays from one of three positions: slave of God, servant of God, or son of God. The slave prays out of fear of punishment; the servant prays out of a desire for reward; but the son prays out of pure love and a desire to do God's will. When one prays out of love it is possible to train the mind to pray constantly.

However, there is the concern that apathy or fixedness can set in and this needs to be resisted. We must get in the habit of weighing each thought to see if it is worthy, just as a money changer examines each coin. In similar fashion we must constantly be assessing what material our minds are processing just as a miller wants fine grain running through his mill, not rocks or mud. Additionally we must check to make sure our thoughts and prayers are floating always upward toward God, untethered by the weight of sin. A wet feather is held to the earth, but a dry feather floats freely.

Recall above all we must strive to be normal humans so, as Augustine said, "our souls can do their natural thing which is to seek God." Accordingly, excessive striving after anything worldly blocks us from being normal and from moving naturally toward God. In prayer, the person must "let go" and allow himself to be "thrown back completely on God." This emphasis is consistent with Cassian's love for the beginning of the 70th Psalm, which reads, "Oh come and rescue me God... Yahweh come quickly and help me!"

Prayer is not a time to reason about worldly things. Prayer is the time you are speaking with and being with your Father. This is not to say you are in a mystical state, you are simply in the presence of your father... Prayer goes through stages just as a person moves from slavery to sonship. The first stage is praying to seek pardon for sin, then one requests spiritual confidence or comfort, then on to prayer for the needs of others, and finally prayer in thanksgiving.

From any of the four preceding states of prayer, Cassian says you might be transported suddenly to a mystical level. But such an experience is strictly in the hands of God. Merton says he feels such transports are usually for only a minute or two. Cassian calls these transports fiery experiences and there are times when a person, in the grip of mystical prayer, has been to known to groan or sigh.

While in prayer, time can be an indeterminate thing. Many people have lost track of time while praying, either in normal prayer or in mystical prayer.

St. John Cassian's reputation suffered during the reformation period. Cassian's views are nuanced. They were not well suited for the "black and white" debates that characterized the reformation era. His writings, particularly his *Institutes & Conferences*, were widely read in the early medieval period, but fell into obscurity after the Reformation. In recent decades, St. John Cassian has experienced something of a revival.

# A Note from Hugh Murray

Dear Readers,

Thank you for reading this book. I hope it increases your knowledge of and interest in the Catholic Church. Please share it with others so they too can learn about this divinely created institution that exists under the protection of the Holy Spirit.

However, the Catholic Church is operated by humans and therefore... possessed of many human flaws.

If you have any questions, comments, or suggestions about this book or the Catholic faith, please feel free to email me at hvm@aol.com. I look forward to hearing from you.

Sincerely,
Hugh Murray

# About the Author

Hugh Murray has always been interested in religion and, unlike many people, feels religion has a place in most conversations. A graduate of Catholic grade school and high school, he's been a member of Jesuit-led discussion groups for more than 50 years. He made his career in business and engineering, but religion has played a large role his entire life.

Murray's passion for history—Europe, the Jews and Christians, and more recently Islam—comes from his mother, whose deep personal faith and curiosity about history (she pursued a doctorate in European History) was instilled in her children at an early age.

As American society has become more secular, Murray has become less secular, learning more and more about his favorite subjects. His book, *Understanding Catholicism*, is the product of his lifelong pursuits.

# Acknowledgements

I would like to thank those who helped form me in my Catholic faith:

My parents, my godparents, my sister and brothers, my aunts, uncles, and cousins, my grade school and high school teachers, my Catholic fraternity brothers from college, the many Manresan Society members and moderators I encountered over 52 years of attending monthly meetings, and the many individual loving, engaged priests and nuns I encountered over a life of 77 years while living in a dozen different parishes.

All of these helped shape my unique view of the Catholic faith.

I would also like to acknowledge the hundreds of good, non-Catholic Christians, Jews, and non-believers I've encountered whom I love and feel would benefit from some knowledge of the Catholic faith, even if they never embrace it. I wrote this book for them... and for you.

# Bibliography (and suggested sources for those wishing to learn more)

**Books:**

*A History of Christianity*, by Paul Johnson, PhD, 1976.

*The Thirty-Five Doctors of the Church*, by Christopher Rengers O.F.M., 2014.

*The General Councils: A History of the Twenty-One Church Councils from Nicaea to Vatican II*, by Christopher M. Bellitto, 2002.

*Catechism of the Catholic Church*, commissioned by Pope John Paul II, 1994.

*Report from the Synod: John Paul II and the Battle for Vatican II*, by Richard Cowden-Guido, 1986.

*Summa Theologica*, by Thomas Aquinas, ~1260.

*The City of God* and *The Confessions*, by Augustine of Hippo, ~ 420.

*The New Catholic Study Bible* (St Jerome edition), 1985.

*Index of Leading Catholic Indicators: The Church since Vatican II*, by Kenneth C. Jones, 2003.

**Online and Mail Order Courses:**

*The Orthodox Christian Church: History, Belief, and Practices*, by Peter Bouteneff, PhD, mail order course available from Now You Know Media, Inc.

*The Council of Trent: Answering the Reformation and Reforming the Church*, by John O'Malley, S.J., PhD, mail order course available from Now You Know Media, Inc.

*Vatican II*, by John O'Malley, S.J., PhD, mail order course available from Now You Know Media, Inc.

*Thomas Merton on Contemplation*, by Thomas Merton with introduction by Fr. Anthony Ciorra, PhD, mail order course available from Now You Know Media, Inc.

*The Catholic Church: A History*, William Cook, PhD, online course available from the Teaching Company. Course No. 6640.

*History of Christian Theology*, Phillip Cary, PhD, online course available from the Teaching Company. Course No. 6450.

*History of Christianity in the Reformation Era*, by Brad Gregory, PhD, online course from the Teaching Company, course No. 690.

*Great Minds of the Medieval World*, Professor Dorsey Armstrong, online course from the Teaching Company. Course No. 4631.

### Encyclopedia articles and websites of interest:

www.catholicstand.com can be used to confirm quotes.

www.wikipedia.org has generally complete and accurate write-ups on each of the Church's important saints.

www.sspx.org has detailed information about the Society of St. Pius X.

www.regnumchristi.org/en/ for more information on the Legionaries of Christ.

Made in the USA
Lexington, KY
31 January 2019